PROJECT: STEAM

MODEL MAKERS

LISA J. AMSTUTZ

Rourke
Educational Media

rourkeeducationalmedia.com

Before & After Reading Activities

Before Reading:

Building Academic Vocabulary and Background Knowledge

Before reading a book, it is important to tap into what your child or students already know about the topic. This will help them develop their vocabulary, increase their reading comprehension, and make connections across the curriculum.

1. *Look at the cover of the book. What will this book be about?*
2. *What do you already know about the topic?*
3. *Let's study the Table of Contents. What will you learn about in the book's chapters?*
4. *What would you like to learn about this topic? Do you think you might learn about it from this book? Why or why not?*
5. *Use a reading journal to write about your knowledge of this topic. Record what you already know about the topic and what you hope to learn about the topic.*
6. *Read the book.*
7. *In your reading journal, record what you learned about the topic and your response to the book.*
8. *After reading the book complete the activities below.*

Content Area Vocabulary
Read the list. What do these words mean?

arches
architecture
biosphere
blueprint
braces
capstone
compression
kinetic energy
mural
paleontologists
potential energy
prototype
scale
tension
trusses
virtual
weathered

After Reading:

Comprehension and Extension Activity

After reading the book, work on the following questions with your child or students in order to check their level of reading comprehension and content mastery.

1. *What is modeling? (Summarize)*
2. *How do models help architects design buildings? (Infer)*
3. *Name one way that biologists use models. (Asking Questions)*
4. *Do you know anyone who builds models as part of their job? (Text to Self Connection)*
5. *What are some different types of models? (Asking Questions)*

Extension Activity

Think about a project you would like to do or something you'd like to learn about. Maybe you're planning to rearrange your room or build a skateboard ramp. Or maybe you want to learn how the water cycle works. How could creating a model help you achieve your goal? What kind of model could you build?

TABLE OF CONTENTS

MODEL MAKERS

Making models can be a fun hobby. But many people also use models in their work. Scientists, architects, engineers, and artists all make models to test their ideas.

A model can be a drawing, a concept, a math equation, a computer program, or a physical object. Foam, plastics, and paper are often used to create lightweight, realistic-looking models. Your cell phone, dishwasher, car, and tennis shoes probably started off as models. Someone might have even modeled the sandwich you ate for lunch!

SPECIAL EFFECTS IN THE ARTS

One well-known model-making studio is Industrial Light & Magic. You may have seen their work in the Star Wars, Harry Potter, or Pirates of the Caribbean films.

BUILDING BRIDGES

What shapes do you see in bridges? Triangles, **arches**, and domes are often used in **architecture** because they are especially strong and stable. **Braces**, or beams set at an angle, are used to make corners stronger.

Many forces act on a bridge. Weight pressing downward causes a force called **compression**. The underside of the bridge experiences a stretching force called **tension**. Engineers carefully design bridges to spread out these forces evenly. That way they do not break the bridge in two.

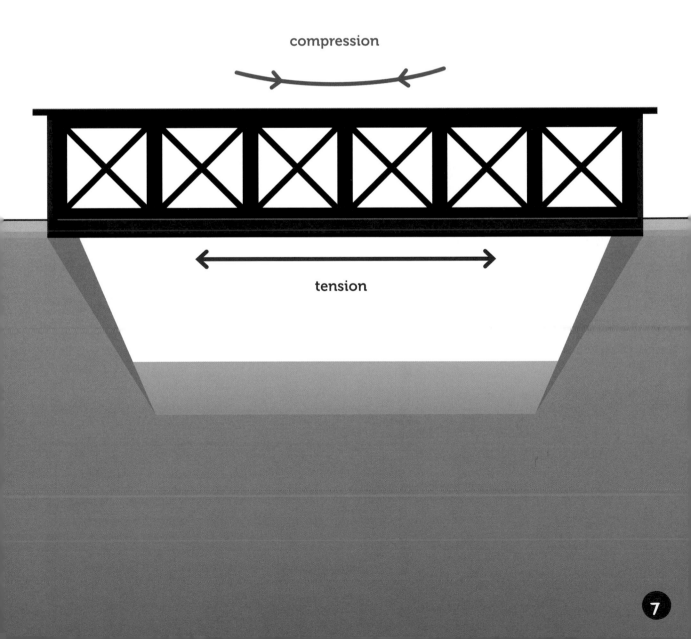

compression

tension

Activity: Build a Bridge

Try using Lego bricks to create a model bridge. Then test the strength of your design. What can you do to make it stronger? Hint: Try adding **trusses** or arches to your model.

> A truss is a wood or metal latticework that helps spread out the forces of compression and tension on a bridge and makes it stronger. An arch spreads out the forces of tension on the underside of a bridge.

Gather:

1. building bricks (Legos or similar)

2. cup

3. weights (marbles or coins work well)

Do:

1. Use building bricks to design a simple bridge.

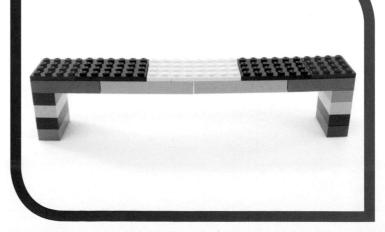

2. Set the cup on the center of the bridge. Gradually add weights to the cup. Note how many you can add before the bridge collapses.

3. Try adding a support to the middle of your bridge. Test it again. Then add braces. Now how much can it hold?

4. Experiment with different shapes: triangles, rectangles, squares, and arches.

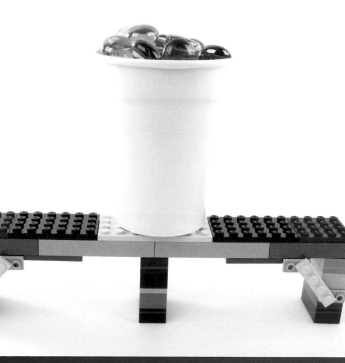

DESIGNING DREAM HOUSES

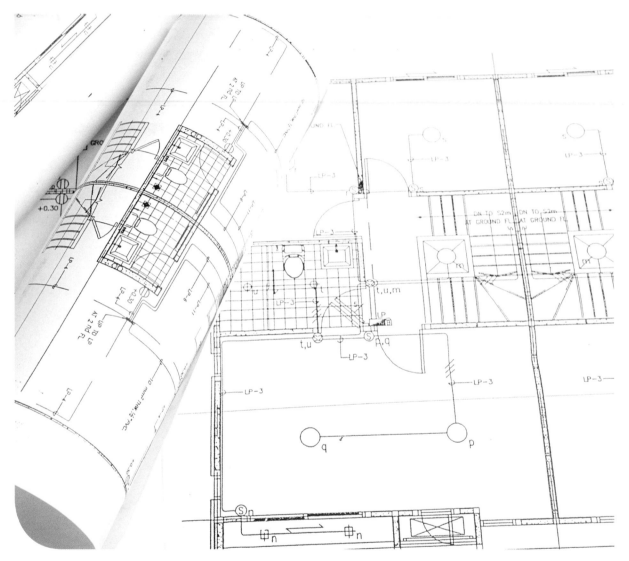

Architects create detailed plans on paper for their designs. These 2D plans may be drawn by hand or by using a computer-aided design (CAD) program. This technology makes it easy to share and edit designs. CAD programs can also create **virtual** 3D designs. That way, a client can tour the building before a single brick is laid!

Architects often create 3D models out of foam core, cardboard, or chipboard for large, costly buildings. These models help their clients picture the finished product.

A 2D, or two-dimensional, model is flat. It has length and width, but not height. A 3D, or three-dimensional, model has height as well.

Activity: Model Your Dream House

Have you ever dreamed of living in a castle? Or is a houseboat or a yurt more your style? Sketch out a floor plan for your dream house. Then create a 3D model.

DRAWING To SCALE

It would not be practical to draw a **blueprint** the same size as the building it represents. That's why architects draw their plans to **scale**. A short distance on the drawing represents a larger distance on the building.

Gather:

1. paper (grid paper works well)

2. glue

3. paint or markers

4. foam core or cardboard

5. ruler

6. pencil

Do:

1. Decide how big you want your house to be. Choose a scale for your drawing so it will fit on the page.

2. Sketch out the layout for your house. Don't forget to leave room for hallways, closets, and bathrooms!

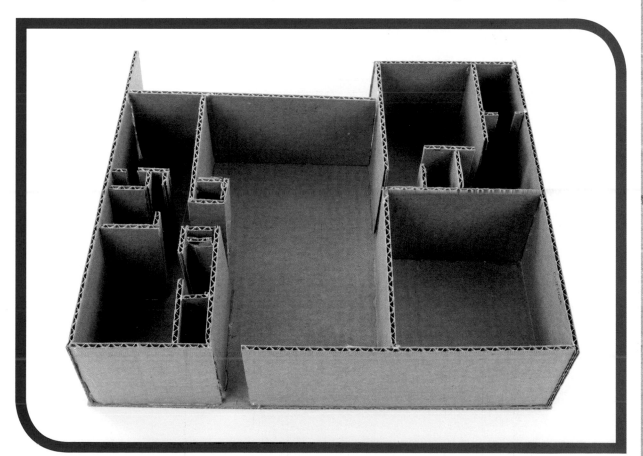

3. Try building a 3D model of your drawing. Cut cardboard or foam core pieces to build the walls. Use the same scale as in your drawing, or enlarge it.

4. Decorate your walls with paint or markers, then glue them together.

CONSTRUCTING DOMES

A geodesic dome looks like half a soccer ball. Most geodesic structures take this form. One of the most well-known geodesic structures, however, Disney's Spaceship Earth, is a complete geodesic sphere. It is made up of more than 11,000 triangles.

Let's say you need a dwelling that can withstand heavy snow, earthquakes, and high winds. What kind of structure should you build?

Hmm ... How about a geodesic dome?

A geodesic dome is made out of triangles. They fit neatly together to create a strong and efficient structure. Some geodesic domes have stood for decades near the South Pole!

TRY THIS

With an adult's help, hot glue craft sticks together to form a rectangle and a triangle. Once the glue has hardened, press down on each shape until it breaks. Which shape could withstand more force?

Activity: Design a Dome

Gather:

1. gumdrops

2. toothpicks

Do:

1. Build a triangle using toothpicks. Use gumdrops to connect the ends together.

2. Add two toothpicks to one of the sides and use a gumdrop to attach them at the top, forming a second triangle.

3. Continue adding triangles in this way until you have created a dome or sphere.

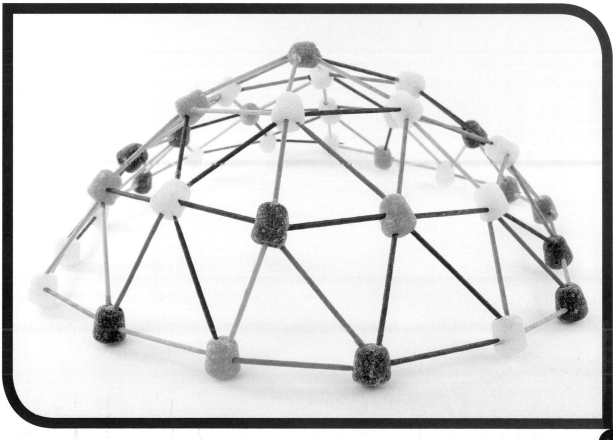

PLANNING PYRAMIDS

Pyramids consist of four triangles leaned against each other. This shape is the most stable way to stack heavy materials like stone or brick, as Egyptian engineers discovered thousands of years ago.

The ancient Egyptians built giant stone pyramids as burial sites for royal families. These structures took decades to build. Many were coated in white limestone and topped with a gold **capstone**. Thousands of years later, the pyramids are **weathered** by sun and wind, but still standing.

Activity: Build a Model Pyramid

Build this model pyramid using sugar cubes.

Gather:

1. 90 sugar cubes

2. glue dots

3. gold paint (optional)

4. gold glitter (optional)

5. paintbrush

6. cardboard

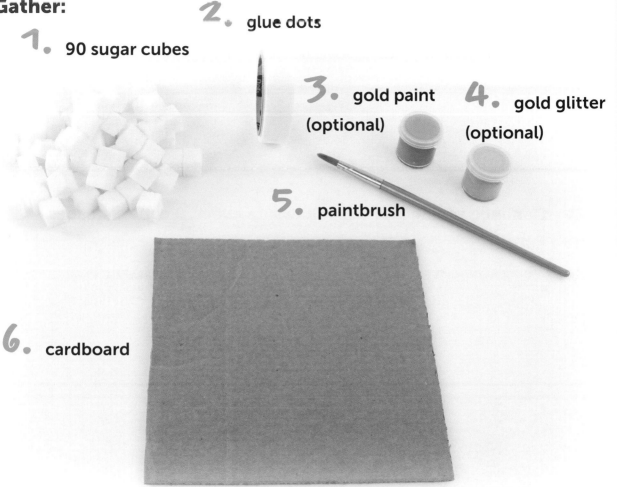

Do:

1. Lay out 36 sugar cubes in a square on a piece of cardboard. Then remove one cube to leave a space for a door. Attach the cubes to the cardboard with glue dots.

2. Glue down 25 sugar cubes in a square on top of the base.

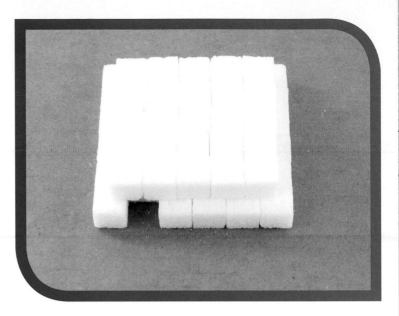

3. Continue adding layers as follows: 16 cubes, 9 cubes, 4 cubes, and 1 cube.

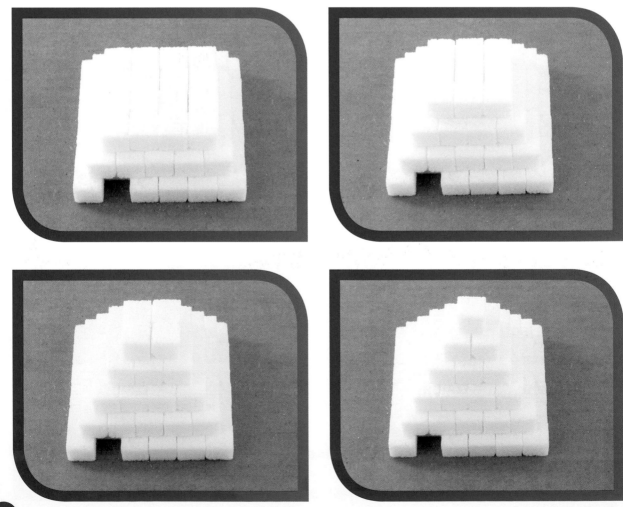

4. Optional: Paint the top cube gold. While the paint is still wet, sprinkle it with glitter. Let it dry before gluing it to the pyramid.

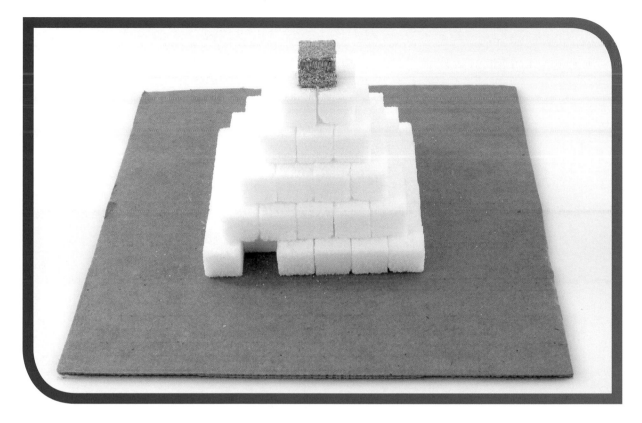

5. Optional: Try building a Mayan pyramid.

Mayan pyramid

IMAGINING DINOS

Paleontologists use models to figure out how prehistoric animals might have looked. These models can be as small as toys. Or they can be life-sized, like the models you see in museums. Some are computer-generated.

3D PRINTERS

Scientists can use 3D printers to make copies of fossils—even those buried in rock. First, a CT scanner is used to x-ray the rock. The image is then sent to a printer. Tiny fossils can be enlarged to make them easier to study, while giant ones can be shrunk to a manageable size.

Activity: Design a Dino

Design a new species of dinosaur. Come up with a name for your dino. Spotosaurus? Gigantosaur?

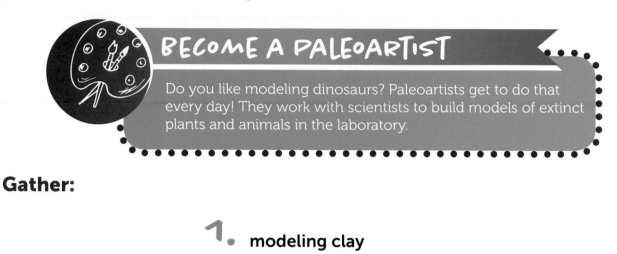

BECOME A PALEOARTIST

Do you like modeling dinosaurs? Paleoartists get to do that every day! They work with scientists to build models of extinct plants and animals in the laboratory.

Gather:

1. **modeling clay**

2. **3D printer software (optional)**

3. **3D printer (optional)**

Do:

1. Using modeling clay, design a dinosaur. Make sure its body is strong enough to stand and well-balanced.

2. Give your dino some flair. Add spots, stripes, swirls, or camouflage.

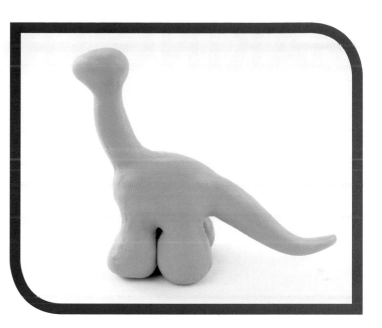

3. Optional: If you have access to a 3D printer program, design a virtual dinosaur.

4. Print your model using a 3D printer.

MAKING TRACKS

Building a roller coaster is a big challenge. Engineers must balance safety with enough speed, height, and turns for maximum thrill. They must calculate the mass of the train, the force required to pull it uphill, its maximum and minimum speed, and many other factors.

Chain loops turned by a motor pull a roller coaster uphill. When it reaches the peak, it has lots of **potential energy**. This turns into **kinetic energy** as the force of gravity pulls the cars downward and forward.

Activity: Build a Roller Coaster

Try your hand at designing the perfect roller coaster! Plan your design on paper and then build a computer model.

Gather:

1. paper
2. ruler
3. pencil
4. roller coaster design program (available online)

Do:

1. Sketch out your roller coaster on paper. Make a note of your scale (1:100, 1:500, etc.)

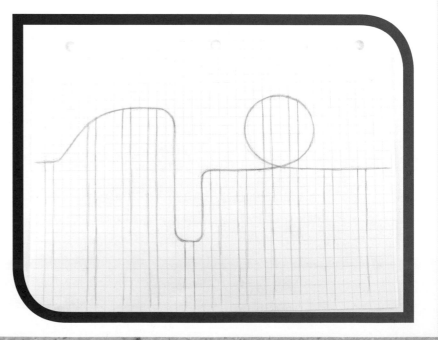

2. Find a roller coaster design program online.

3. Use the design you created on paper to build a computer model.

4. Test out your model. How well did it work?

CREATING FURNITURE

A **prototype** is an early model from which other forms are developed. Inventors often make prototypes of items they want to produce.

Furniture makers often create models of their new designs. Placing them into model buildings shows how they will look and fit in the space.

Activity: Model Furniture

Use cardboard boxes and tubes to create model furniture for a dollhouse or display. Try to match the scale of the space so the furniture will look proportional.

Gather:

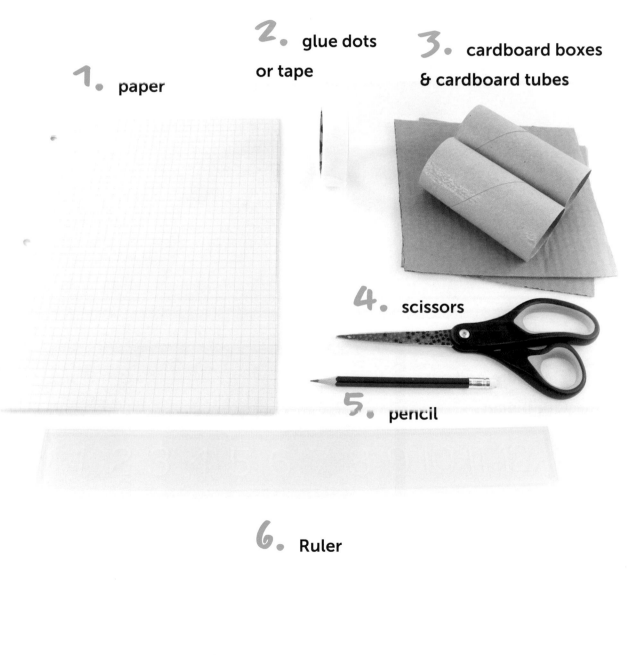

2. glue dots or tape

3. cardboard boxes & cardboard tubes

1. paper

4. scissors

5. pencil

6. Ruler

Do:

1. Sketch out your design.

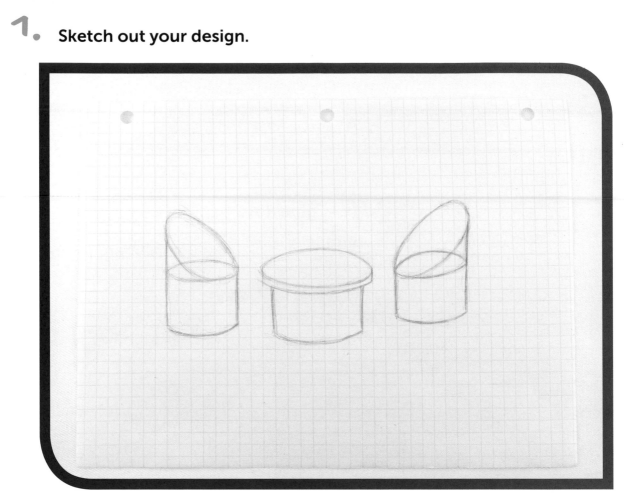

2. Measure and cut out your pieces.

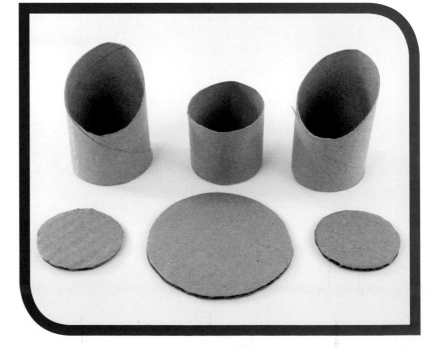

3. Decorate your furniture as desired.

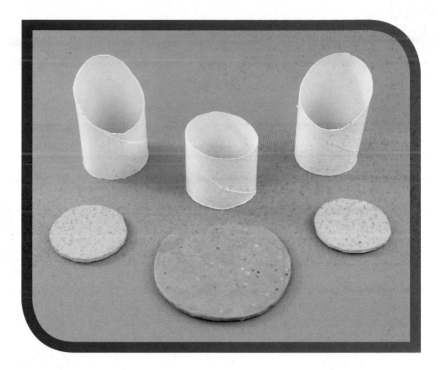

4. Glue or tape together each piece of furniture.

MURAL MODELING

To create a large wall mural, artists can use a grid system, draw directly on the wall, or project a design with an overhead projector.

Models come in handy when an artist is planning a large project such as a **mural** or sculpture. They allow the artist to test materials and envision the final project. This saves money and time.

Activity: Make a Mural

Create a mural by transferring a sketch to a larger sheet of paper. This technique can be used to copy or resize many kinds of drawings.

Gather:

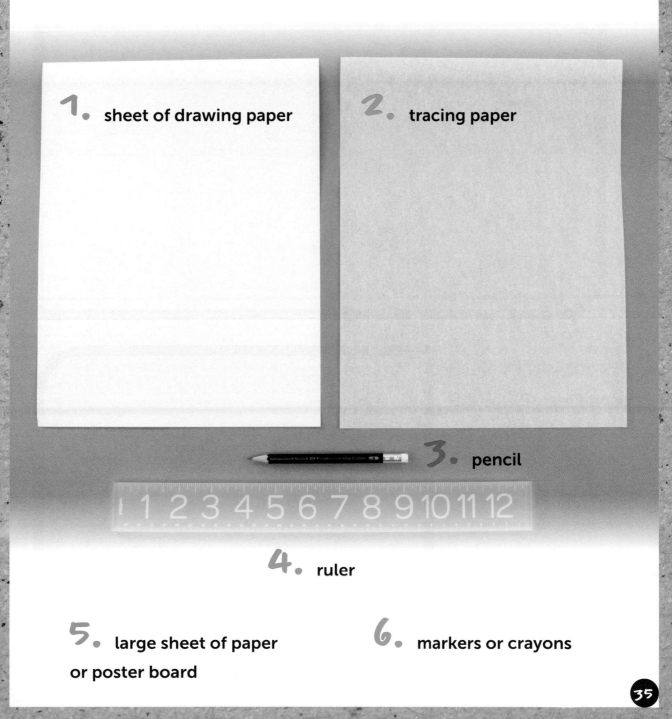

1. **sheet of drawing paper**

2. **tracing paper**

3. **pencil**

4. **ruler**

5. **large sheet of paper or poster board**

6. **markers or crayons**

Do:

1. On the smaller sheet of paper, sketch out your design.

2. Draw a one inch by one inch (2.5 by 2.5 centimeter) grid on the sheet of tracing paper. Lay it over your design.

3. Draw a larger grid on the large sheet of paper or poster board. You need the same number of squares as you have on your tracing paper.

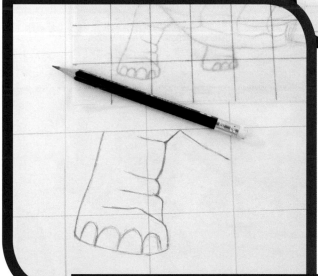

4. Starting in one corner, draw the shape you see in each square of the small grid onto the corresponding square of the larger grid. Continue copying each square until your drawing is completed.

5. Color your mural.

BUILDING SKYSCRAPERS AND TOWERS

Designing buildings is both an art and a science. Architects and civil engineers often work together to create structures that are attractive, safe, and strong.

A tower needs a wide, strong base to give it support. It must be perfectly balanced so it doesn't fall over in the first strong wind. The Eiffel Tower in Paris, France was the tallest building in the world when it was built in the late 1880s. The arches at its base give it support

At this time, the world's tallest building is the Burj Khalifa in Dubai, United Arab Emirates. It is 2,717 feet (828 meters) tall and has 163 floors.

Activity: Erect an Eiffel Tower

Use craft sticks to create a model of the Eiffel Tower. Then try modeling the Leaning Tower of Pisa or the Space Needle!

Gather:

1. craft sticks

2. hot glue gun or glue dots

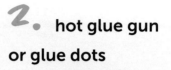

Do:

1. Create four arches as pictured.

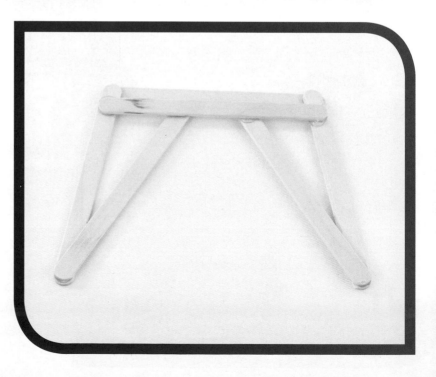

2. Glue the arches together in a square. Ask an adult to help if you use a hot glue gun.

3. Lay craft sticks across the top to create a platform.

4. Now build the rest of the tower.

MODELING NATURE

In 1991, scientists completed a giant biological model known as Biosphere 2. This 3.14-acre (1.27-hectare) structure contained five different biomes. A team of eight people sealed themselves inside for two years to test the model. Biosphere 2 is now open to the public for tours.

Biologists often create models to show how a process works in nature. Models can explain how genes, cells, and brains work. They can show how plants or viruses grow or how organisms relate to each other in an ecosystem. Many of these models are now built on computers.

Activity: Build a Biosphere

Earth's ecological systems and all the organisms in them are called the **biosphere**. Create a model biosphere in a jar and watch it grow! The water in the jar will evaporate, then condense and run back down the sides. As long as the jar remains closed, you should not need to add any water.

Gather:

1. clean jar with a lid

2. gravel

3. activated charcoal

4. moss

5. 1 to 3 small plants

6. potting soil

7. water

8. decorations (natural items or small toys)

Do:

1. Place 1 to 2 inches (2.54 to 5.08 centimeters) of gravel in the bottom of the jar.

2. Layer a half inch (1.27 centimeters) of activated charcoal over the gravel.

3. Top with 3 inches (7.62 centimeters) of potting soil.

4. Add the plants. Press soil around the plants to hold them in place.

5. Cover the remaining soil surface with moss.

6. Water the plants. The soil should be damp but not soggy.

7. Add decorations.

8. Screw the lid tightly onto the jar. Set it near a sunny window.

GLOSSARY

arches (ARCH-ez): curved shapes that are often used in architecture

architecture (AR-ki-tek-chur): the profession of designing buildings

biosphere (BAHY-uhs-feer): the part of Earth's surface and atmosphere that supports life

blueprint (BLOO-print): a detailed plan or drawing of a structure

braces (BRAYS-ez): beams that support or steady a structure

capstone (KAP-stone): the top stone in a structure

compression (kuhm-PRE-shuhn): the force pressing or pushing on a structure

kinetic energy (ki-NET-ik EN-ur-jee): the energy of an object in motion

mural (MYU-ruhl): a large-scale picture, often painted on a wall or ceiling

paleontologists (pale-ee-uhn-TOL-uh-jists): scientists who study fossils

potential energy (puh-TEN-shuhl EN-ur-jee): energy stored in an object

prototype (PROH-tuh-tipe): a first model from which later versions are developed

scale (SKALE): a ratio of the size of a model to the full-size object

tension (TEN-shuhn): the force of something stretching or pulling on a structure

trusses (TRUSS-ez): wooden or metal frameworks that support a wall or bridge

virtual (VUR-choo-uhl): existing in a computer program or on the Internet

weathered (WETH-urd): worn down by exposure to the weather

INDEX

SHOW WHAT YOU KNOW

1. Name three jobs that involve making models.
2. How do models help artists create large pieces of art?
3. What does a paleoartist do?
4. Which shapes are the strongest?
5. What is the purpose of a truss on a bridge?

FURTHER READING

Challoner, Jack, *Maker Lab: 28 Super Cool Projects*, DK Children, 2016.

Challoner, Jack, *Maker Lab Outdoors: 25 Super Cool Projects*, DK Children, 2018.

Graves, Colleen and Graves, Aaron, *The Big Book of Makerspace Projects: Inspiring Makers to Experiment*, Create, and Learn, McGraw-Hill Education, 2016.

ABOUT THE AUTHOR

Lisa Amstutz is the author of more than 80 books for kids. She specializes in topics related to science and agriculture. Lisa's background includes a B.A. in Biology and an M.S. in Environmental Science. She lives with her family on a small farm in Ohio. Learn more at her website: www.LisaAmstutz.com.

www.rourkeeducationalmedia.com

PHOTO CREDITS: Cover & Pages 8, 9, 12, 13, 16, 17, 19, 20, 21, 24, 25, 28, 31, 32, 33, 35, 36, 37, 40, 41, 43, 44, 45: © creativelytara; Page 4: © nicolas_; Page 5: © PeopleImages, Elenarts; Page 6: © bluejayphoto; Page 7: © weenee; Page 10: © onairjiiw; Page 11: © jacoblund; Page 14: © Russell102; Page 15: © stickytoffeepudding; Page 18: © Botjan7; Page 21: © cinoby; Page 22: © FreerLaw; Page 23: © kynny, czgur; Page 26: © Philartphace; Page 27: © zennie; Page 29: © chaofann; Page 30: © Marco Rosario Venturini Auteri; Page 34: © zodebala; Page 38: © Drazen Lauric; Page 39: © neirfy, dblight; Page 42: © s99

Edited by: Keli Sipperley
Cover and Interior design by: Tara Raymo *www.creativelytara.com*

Library of Congress PCN Data

Model Makers / Lisa J. Amstutz
(Project: STEAM)
ISBN 978-1-64156-461-8 (hard cover)(alk. paper)
ISBN 978-1-64156-587-5 (soft cover)
ISBN 978-1-64156-703-9 (e-Book)
Library of Congress Control Number: 2018930487

Printed in the United States of America, North Mankato, Minnesota

Rourke Educational Media
Printed in the United States of America,
North Mankato, Minnesota